AF353571

publisher a
sumed for (
ion contai

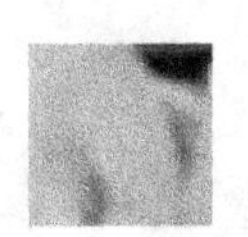

D,LECT
)R SECO
PUR SAI

forts col

graced.

ce,

ak,

nvoy,

n,
un;

'umanit

ch adhe

rd

and chi

n
sacred

eal

·h to ove·

anxiety

asm
l bath.

ner grai

saddes

ry,

reed,
od and f

for any

it's day

life.

hind.

ire and

ımanity

ch other

beautif

ıe nectaı

ot mome
of dew,

on.

ague

ed side.

ued ever

der

be

omplish.

scena.

h are mc

ir

d again

e aroun

to feel l

our smi

:ind, feel

he sun n

ariot of

ble whic

strong

rm on h

child h

www.ingramcontent.com/pod-product-compliance
Lightning Source LLC
LaVergne TN
LVHW011603210726
843509LV00016BA/839